I0200943

Never Retire God

By: Donnetta Austin

Copyright 2017 by the author of this book,
Donnetta Austin. This book's author retains
sole copyright to all contributions to this book.

This book, or parts thereof, may not be
reproduced, stored in retrieval systems, or
transmitted in any means or any form without
the written permission of the author.

The author owns the design for the cover as
well.

Published in the United States by
Testimonies of Hope Publishing
PO Box 3951
Rock Island, IL 61204

Library of Congress Cataloging-in
Publication Data

ISBN-13: 978-0-692-88003-6
ISBN-10: 0-692-88003-8

Table of Contents

Introduction

You may feel burned out from many years of hard work and labor. It may even seem as though you are ready to call it quits. Do you hold out a little bit longer, or do you give in?

This book is about how to keep a steady pace and find balance through life's struggles.

Scenario: *The Job Search*

A company you have been interested in offers you a position. They feel as though you are qualified, and the interview goes remarkably well. Most of us think to ourselves, "I'll accept the position and, most likely, start at entry level. I'll work my way up to the level I would like to achieve". As a new employee, you want to show impeccable performance in order to make a good impression.

Some of us may accept a position and stay on the job assignment temporarily. After a while, you get an itch to go look for something else… something better. If you don't think things through and weigh all of your options, you may end up making a poor decision. Considering every option carefully is a necessary process in order to prevent unnecessary cycles. Living inconsistently in the moment and just getting by is not good enough.

On the other hand, if all is going well, some people will stay with a company for a longer term. Some people prefer to remain with a job that is more structured, reliable, and has great benefits. This type of job becomes a comfort zone.

Once you've established yourself, you begin to look for new ways to advance to another level within the same company. You are making progress and headed towards your purpose.

Finally, you've reached your goal you had set in mind. What will you do with all of the profit? What better way than to utilize your prosperity than to share it? Give unto others. And as you gain more, share more!

What gifts do you have in making your testimony transparent to bless others?

A while back, an acquaintance I knew was interested in relocating to a new city. While seeking different job opportunities within their profession, this acquaintance found the process of searching for a full-time position to be quite challenging. It was difficult because all companies ran their systems differently. If you are used to doing things one way for many years, chances are the next office or department will not be the same. You will have to alter your thinking, adapt to your surroundings, and get with the program. So, they decided to go through a temp agency instead.

When you opt to find work through a temp agency, you are asked quite a few questions. These questions relate to your work history and your long-term career plans. How long have you been on your current job? How long have you been searching for a job?

What are your qualifications? Do you specialize in a particular area? What is your desired salary? Are you only interested in temporary work, or would you consider a temp to hire position? Is this your permanent residence? The agency takes all of this information into consideration when deciding to hire you for a specific company.

Usually you are on the job for a specific time frame. For example, a company may need a temporary employee because a full-time employee is on maternity leave. In other instances, a company may go through an agency to seek out someone who is a good fit for a permanent position. The employer looks at how compatible you are with them and the company. If it all goes well, you will be lined up with a company who has a job opening.

In going through this experience, you may find that going through a temp agency is not the best option for you. You may even decide transitioning to a different company is not your best choice. Staying where you are brings comfort and security. Especially, if you have been there for quite some time, and they offer benefits. Most agencies offer you a decent salary or hourly pay rate but no benefits.

How do these decisions affect you later in life? If you abort a season in your life before it's time, you may miss out on a blessing that God was trying to prepare you. In that same respect, you could be staying in a place where your time is up. That will cause you to miss a blessing too. In later chapters, we will examine other areas in life where this may be the case and how to overcome.

Chapter 1

Recognizing Myself
Without Jesus

God gives all of us a choice to live freely. That being said, we are left with two options:

1. Live a life for this world.

2. Live a life for Jesus.

I started off with option one. I did not realize the significance of option two until later in life around the age of 32. Growing up, I thought that there was a phase or a sequence of events that you went through which helped you to reach maturity.

I think that in our childhood years a lot of times we have not fully conceptualized what it means to be responsible. We have yet to develop those decision-making skills. There are even those who may have had to step up early and become a "role model" or adult depending on the circumstances. Even then, you miss out on the opportunity of just being a child and experiencing the stages in life that are meant for you to go through. These folks have to grow up too fast!

As the years go by and we begin to mature, we get exposed to different aspects of life and learn to make choices. We take the situation at hand, contemplate our options, and think to ourselves. At times, one decision may sound good at the moment, but you're not even thinking about what's best in the long run. Ultimately, the decision is left for us to make. In our early age, we like the sound of living in the moment now and being satisfied.

I held onto the idea that you lived under your parent's rules until the time you head off to college. When you begin college, you start to have an idea of what it's like to be a little more independent. It's even possible that you meet the one special guy and end up falling head over heels in love! Everyone seems to notice the huge grin that appears on your face.

A lot of times when women fall in love we get all bubbly, and the man we have fallen for becomes a part of our daily routine. We consider him in every aspect of our life. He becomes ahead or above everything else that is a priority in our lives. Before you know it, several years have passed and we are thinking about marriage, having children, purchasing our first home, and traveling the world. We think to ourselves all is good. Well, WRONG!

Sometimes life can take a detour, and you make a left turn. Living life can be a journey and may not always follow the direction you planned. Have you ever felt like you had everything figured out? In your eyes, the life you had planned was picture perfect. What happened?

Living for the World

Along the way, I decided to do things my own way. I felt like all this time had passed me by, and it meant nothing. My self-esteem was low, I questioned if my standards were too high, and thought maybe I'm just not good enough. I was devastated trying to figure out how to cope with the dysfunction. My heart felt shattered into a million pieces. Every step I would try and move forward seemed so unfamiliar. I quickly became complacent. I was thinking to myself "why me"? Why do I have to be the one forced out of a situation that was not even my fault? All of the chaos in my mind was just a misunderstanding.

While replaying the events that crossed my mind over and over again I came to the realization that this was really happening. It was my reality. But I didn't want to change. I liked the way things were. With a sigh I said to myself, "So be it".

Multiple times I would move backwards trying to rekindle what was lost. I was in denial hoping if I just start over and try to fix my flaws, it will all turn out for the best. Without even realizing it, I was repeating a cycle of desperation. It was so petty, but I would do things to try and get some attention and be noticed. It would make my day to take some time out for me. So, what did I do? I grabbed my purse, along with my credit card, and went on a shopping spree!

Nothing could make me happier at the time than to splurge a little bit. I had a good eye for a particular style and look. Whatever I bought had to be classy but sassy. It has always been easier for me to go look for an outfit first before the accessories. I always looked for color to compliment my skin tone. My whole attire would have to be on point from head to toe. My hair would be in a really cute updo, with a couple of popping kinky curls on the side. My heels and handbag were color coordinated too. I have never really been big on fashion jewelry, but dangling earrings and a bracelet would do. Wearing a necklace would depend on how busy the detail was in my outfit. Oh, and I cannot forget to mention, after that is all said and done, I would have to get my face all dolled up and look flawless with MAC cosmetics. Last but not least, I'd be wearing my favorite scent of perfume. Once I was all put together and freshened, I would be ready for an evening out.

Adding Up the Cost

Believe me when I tell you that it didn't matter if I had the cash for the expenses or not. My credit card always came in handy. I would practically live off of using my credit card not even caring about the cost or interest rate that built up. It was not a problem for me to pay the minimum monthly payments. Sooner than later, my spending habits got out of hand. On more than one occasion, my credit card quickly ran up to a balance of $5,000.00. All it did was give me a headache! I would continually try and keep up with my bills and pay on a credit card that was adding 18 percent interest.   The bank was definitely winning.

My struggle just kept getting worse. It was so hard to catch up. I found myself borrowing money to pay off the card and turning right around to use it again. I even tried to figure out which other bills could be altered so I could pay for the credit card. Even lowering my cell phone bill or cable was not enough to catch up on paying my credit card. It was time for me to get a part-time job.

I found a job or two that worked out temporarily for extra money. The problem was that the positions I picked up were seasonal holiday jobs. The little bit of money I got paid was not enough to save. I would need it for gas to get to and from one job to the other. I would be working my tail off and have nothing to show for it. This situation started to strain me, and it got old real fast. I even got to a point where I felt like I needed to seek advice from a financial advisor.

I finally made an appointment to speak with someone. They wrote out a strategy along with a plan for me to follow. It all sounded good while I was speaking with them in their office, but when I got home it was a different story. A couple days would go by. Then weeks. Then months would pass by without reviewing the forms and utilizing them.

I realized that people could give you great advice all day long. The real key is actually listening to them and putting their advice into action.

Do you see what was happening here? Once again, I was not getting anywhere. I didn't like how I began to recognize myself without true guidance.

Chapter 2

Needing More of Jesus

I was beginning to feel hopeless and like a failure. I tried reaching out for advice and comfort. All I wanted was a peace of mind and for someone to tell me everything was going to be all right.

How do you give hope or encouragement to someone who has lost his or her focus?

The best thing to do in this case is to be compassionate, understanding, show that you care, and let them know you are there with a shoulder to lean on. Maybe their daily routine has become a blur? What do you do? Ask what can you do to help. If you are the person in need, sometimes it may feel as though the weight is too much to bear. You may have to start all over again, and that's ok. Remember, take baby steps and ask

God for his strength.

When you lose something it's normal to go through a grieving process. What are the steps to take to help you through the process of a hardship? Take it one day at a time. Have your moment. Remember to breath. Calm your heart by thinking positive thoughts and good memories.

Ask God for help. Keep Him first and in the midst of your every move. Silent prayers never go unheard. Some days may be harder than others. Each day, however, will be progress in moving forward. Try and stay occupied as much as possible with activities that interest you. Remember the hobbies that brought you joy and ease.

It's also a good idea to make

sure you have a strong network of support. Keep your loved ones close. Also, reach out to your church family, and stay informed about various church programs and events. Eventually, just by being in the presence of God's house, we are able to hear Him and His word.

There are times when you go through a storm, the wind is blowing from every angle, and extreme rain is pouring down on your parade. You just want to vent and tell someone about it- anyone who will listen! Throughout life I have discovered that everyone does not have your best interest in mind.

Have you ever talked to someone and told them about the trials and tribulations you have experienced? After it was all said and done it felt like a huge weight lifted off of your shoulders, right? Then they proceed to tell you what they would do if they were in your shoes. Now, most of us know if the tables were turned they would not be in their right mind either.

I could not possibly be the only one who has been at a loss for words in my situation. My struggles got to a point where loved ones were beginning to worry. I felt somewhat like Paul in the Bible.

Paul experienced hardship in multiple areas of his life. He even went to prison! Like Paul, I was fearful, scared, down and hurting inside. It took me years to find the confidence to believe in myself again. I had to learn to swallow my pride and seek a higher alternative. The one and only "person" who came across my mind was God.

I knew He was bigger than what I was experiencing. When we're feeling this way, it is best to draw ourselves near to God no matter how hard it is to believe in what His word says. Every inch you take counts. This is where option two, "Live a Life for Jesus", started to take mold for me.

Living for Jesus

I was given a gift from someone dear to my heart. The gift was a book called *The Secret Power of Speaking God's Word* by Joyce Meyer. This scripture book helped me through so many sleepless nights. What I particularly appreciated about the book was that the content was broken down by emotion. We all know that our emotions can change from day to day. In the book

I found a variety of emotions I may have been feeling at the time.

This allowed me to look at the emotions I was experiencing and go directly to the page that has related scriptures concerning that emotion. It told me exactly where to find it in the Bible. I felt a sense of encouragement whenever I read a verse from the Bible. Reading daily verses from the Bible can give you hope and the desire to keep pushing forward no matter what the circumstance is.

This was a critical point for me because I had to accept that God's ways are not our ways. He has something much bigger in store for each one of us. It was a challenge for me to learn how to move out of my own way. During this time of trials and tribulations I felt like my thoughts were constantly warring against each other.

It may have taken me some time, but I finally agreed with God that a change needed to happen. I knew that change would have to begin with ME. I clearly heard God speak to my heart. It was as if God was speaking to my inner soul, my spirit. I knew I could not master this obstacle alone.

It dawned on me that God wanted more out of me. He wanted the alone time for Him and I to get to know each other better. He wants a spiritual, close, and intimate type of relationship with all of us.

The change starts by seeking God in every way possible. Some ways to seek God include fasting, prayer, reading the Bible, praise and worship, listening to worship music, attending Bible study or going to Sunday school. You must also apply the Word of God to your life.

There are times when you may even want to watch or listen to a service or two online. I have had a moment of stillness in my heart as well by watching an online program. In this case, I would just call on the name of Jesus hoping He heard my heart cry. Sometimes we experience a moment of being speechless, but believe me. It does not go unnoticed.

I had to remember that while I am seeking God, just go to Him first. Before telling all of my business to any and everyone, I go to God. I go to Him first for advice and Godly counsel. Even though it may feel like the right thing to do by sharing our problems with our neighbors, a lot of times it ends up being destructive.

God knows what is best. When we rush into doing things our way, it holds us back from what God wants for us in the long run. When I think about this phrase, it is a mirror image of myself at times. I can be very stubborn. If I let my thoughts get ahead of me too soon, I am quick to jump into a situation without fully thinking it through.

To keep myself moving in the right direction, I had to continuously feed my mind. I had to do my homework by looking up and learning as much as I could about Jesus.

The more time I set aside and spent with Him, the more He would show Himself to me. Although I thought about my past and the things I could not change, I had a glimpse of my present situation. Because my perspective was changing, things began to turn around. I was finally able to look up rather than feel down.

Chapter 3

Short-Term Inconsistency

Although I could see the changes happening in my life, it was also easy for me to fall back into my old habits. My emotions were all over the place. They would change from one minute to the next. I remember the pity parties and feeling sorry for myself. I would have moments of thinking nothing is ever going to change. This process sometimes brought me back to memories I did not want to retrace again.

Everything in my path would bother me. For example, let's examine how I would watch movies. I would decide on a particular title and be intrigued at the beginning. The movie would have my full attention. I would be focused to the point where you would have thought I had a role in the film. I mean, sometimes I really felt like I could be a part of the cast!

One particular movie touched my heart because some of the scenes were close to home. They were so relatable; it was like I was having deja'vu. Yes, I could relate to several of the characters. Of course, my emotions were being stirred up by these movies from my own personal experiences. Every part of me was trying to hold it together and not get unglued.

Even though I wanted to lose my cool, I had to look around and remember where I was. I was usually home on my couch watching Netflix on my TV screen. I thought to myself, "Yeah. It's time for me to maintain and keep a calm attitude". I had to remember not to let my emotions get the best of me in the movie as well as in life. I knew very well that if I did let my emotions take over, I would fall back into the trap of discouragement.

With fear of falling back into the same cycle, I began to plead with God to give me another chance. I promised Him I would do better. And in one minute, my disposition would turn around with a still small voice in my ear telling me, "I got this". Then I heard another whisper saying, "I cannot do this!" I started to drift away and everything came to a halt.

God does not want us to just go to Him when it's convenient for us. He wants us to be able to approach Him boldly with our prayers and requests. He wants this not just some of the time, but all of the time. Make Him a priority before anything else in life. God hears and knows our thoughts before we even bring it to His attention. It is important to come to Him whole-heartedly rather than in total anger or frustration. There is a way of having our prayers heard without demanding them.

When we lose all control of our emotions, believe me, God will let us have our moment or temper tantrum. It will not make Him move or answer our prayer request any sooner than in His timing. When we learn to calm down, become vulnerable, and pour our soul out to Him, that is when in the stillness of our heart and "spirit" we will hear Him. If your heart, mind, and soul are not still, you will not hear from God. You'll be too distracted.

Chapter 4

Longevity

The Lord is with us for the long haul. He said, "I will never leave you nor forsake you". Meaning, the Lord is with us always and will never fail us.

God's love is everlasting. He is who He says He is. He is our provider, healer, comforter, strength, overseer, almighty God, and the One. The One who is able to do all things and turns all of my worries, concerns, and sorrows into joy. He can take all of your bad days and turn them into better days. The Lord God is my friend. He walks and talks with me through the valleys of life and cures all of my troubles. He is my comforter and companion in the time of need. There is no one like Him.

The yearning of my soul craves Him. I need Him every second, minute, and hour of the day. There is not a day that goes by that I don't cherish each and every moment spent with Him. Every day we awake is a gift, and we shall not forget it.

I believe that there is nothing in the world that can be compared to the blessing and gift of a personal relationship with God. He Himself is enough. Just the thought of having someone love us as His children as much as He does is an incredible, joyous, and indescribable feeling. Think about it. We really don't have to want or need for anything. We are never without. He provides enough for all of us to experience His love, grace, and mercy at any given time. All it takes is one call out to Him to embrace his presence. He takes us in just as we are. There are no ands, ifs, or buts about it.

Do you know where I've come from? It took a lot to let go of my yesterdays. There was a lot of shame, guilt, and hurt. The beat of my heart used to race rapidly while chasing after the desires of my flesh. It always led to harm. I had to learn to say "No". The enemy is a liar! Now, I talk back to the enemy. I strongly affirm, "No, you can't steal the joy I have! Lord, I choose you".

There may be times that I don't understand circumstances going on in my life, but God's love outweighs it all. If it's one thing I have learned to do through the ups and downs, it is to trust in God. No matter what comes my way I still have my Lord. At the end of the day,

God is everything to me.

He is everything I have always imagined. I know for sure that I am better off with God in my life than I could ever be without Him. I also know that if it were not for my past, I would not be the woman I am today.

I never would have thought by telling my story it could possibly make a difference in someone else's life. I hope that it has. I pray that my testimony gets passed along to many people across the world for encouragement. Each and every one of us all go through disappointing times in our lives. I chose to overcome mine by seeking God.

I wanted to develop a habit of being more like you, Jesus, and less like me. Things of this world do nothing for me long-term. They may satisfy my flesh for a bit, but they leave nothing left in the end, but an empty soul. See, you have to become familiar with who you were back then, compared to who you are now.

How do you see yourself?

I know I've been changed. What will help me to prosper in the long run is knowing that God is in control, and He has the whole world in the palms of his hand. You see, by stepping out on faith we can trust that what is meant to be will be. If it's not meant to be, the door will close for our good.

Chapter 5

*Building
Interest & Purpose*

In my eyes, what I once saw was a lost soul. Now, I have been found through Christ who strengthens me each and everyday. He has placed on my heart the desire to always seek Him and know that through His knowledge and wisdom, dreams will follow. I have discovered that I have the ability to either let my weakness have control over me or let God's strength heal and cure me. It's by God's grace and mercy that He gives me chance after chance to come to Him with baggage, concerns, and everything else. I surrender and fully realize I have nothing left but God.

It is only through having this faith in God, that in the end, I still have hope. I have hope in spite of my past and things not turning out the way I thought it would. In my heart, I know in due time blessings will be on the way!

Like David in the Bible, I have to remember to walk by faith and not by sight. We may not know what is ahead, but we can be sure that God takes full responsibility when we obey Him and trust in His will for our lives.

One thing I have noticed about myself is that it has taken many years for me to realize how important a relationship with God is. I have grown in ways that would not be possible to do on my own. No matter how many times I slip backwards into old habits or my old way of thinking. The Lord seems to always make a way, and He grabs my attention pulling me back on track.

Communicate with God

Lord, I live for you. To hear your voice speaking truth and promises to my ear, spirit and soul is dear. I think of you as my heavenly father. You are the One I can call on and confide. I am able to share my innermost secrets with you. I am thankful and can trust the fact that you'll never expose them or look at me differently for being flawed. You love me endlessly as your daughter, and you want nothing but the best for my life. I adore you and appreciate all you do for me. Thank you for your patience and for being steadfast.

You are my friend. You are the One who can relate to me through the many obstacles and experiences I've been through. I can step outside of my comfort zone leaping into an adventure of faith knowing you are right beside me. You keep me company during the times I feel alone. When I am out of character and need to vent, you give me a new perspective putting me back in line.

We have a great bond, and we know each other well. I cherish moments of joy shared between us. With a smile on my face, I have to say, "You are alright by me"!

As my counselor, teacher, and instructor, I come to you needing advice. You take me in with open arms when I need to be re-directed. At times there are many tests I have to take. I even have to re-take some of those tests until I pass them and fully understand the purpose behind them.

You lead me to a path of significance even when I don't understand my way. I have to keep in mind how detrimental it can be to simply take a short cut. Is it really worth it? Or would I rather learn from the mistake and correct it? Sometimes it's easy to get into a rush and want things out of instant gratification. The truth is, nothing worthwhile happens overnight. For most of us, it takes a positive mindset along with endurance and dedication to wait for God's best.

Lord, you have a way of healing. You have a way of making everything alright. When we fall, you are right by our side giving us the strength to get back up and try again. You have a way of easing the pain when life becomes too much to bear. There is no other person I know to run to who can sympathize and give comfort the way you do. Lord, I don't know how you do it. You have a lot on your plate. All of us need you in some way, shape, or form.

You have an enormous variety of issues and concerns going on in this world. It's amazing how you are able to balance and carry all of the weight in the palm of your hand.

You are the ultimate Provider! Here is an acronym for you, Lord, as our Provider.

P stands for "provider". God is our provider for any and everything needed in our lives.

R stands for "relationship". There is no relationship as stable as the one He freely offers to us.

O stands for "obstacles". There will be many hurdles to jump and to overcome in our lives, but there is only one in which we can truly always rely.

V stands for "victorious". You can overcome anything with a positive mindset and hope. Keep in mind the sweet reminder in Philippians 4:13, "I can do all things through Christ who strengthens me", and you'll win every time!

I stands for "indulge". Allow yourself to consider getting to know God. Once you do, you will not regret it. Indulge in every occasion with Him.

D stands for "deliverer". He follows through with what He says He would do. We must listen closely believing in His word and promises.

E stands for "endurance". Everything worthwhile goes through a period that challenges our patience and endurance.

R stands for "renew". No matter what, we are given another chance time and time again.

Finding Purpose

Today, my heart still desires to one day get married, have children, and live with a purpose to make a difference in someone's life. It is clearer to me today than it has ever been. This too shall come to pass. It is definitely not the end of my story. It is just the beginning.

I have taken this time of singleness to grow. I have grown closer in my relationship with God, healed from my past, learned to smell the flowers, jump for joy and love myself again. Yes, I have learned to smile again!

I can lift my head high with confidence again. There is no better feeling than to let go of the butterflies that once were a cramp in my stomach from all of the pain and hurt that I was used to.

Learn to let go and let God. It is something I should have learned how to do a long time ago. Remember, it is never too late to start. Why wait? A lot of us are good at procrastinating, but what good does that do? The longer you wait, the longer it will be in finding out what God has in store for you.

How important is it for you to live a life for Jesus? You must believe that it's urgent! Are you willing to sacrifice? I am a firm believer that I am nothing without the Almighty God. Yes, I am ready to live my life for Jesus and stop making it about me. I encourage you to do the same.

Lord, I lift your name on high. I sing and praise your holy name.

Singing…

I need thee oh I need thee. Every hour I need thee. Oh, bless me now my savior. I come to thee.

God, my heart is so relieved knowing that you are here with us. Time passes us in a blink of an eye, but the clock continues ticking. We continue growing and learning.

Father God, I've come to realize how important it is to come together, forgive, and to share.

We must first forgive ourselves and then others. Forgive for being so hard on yourself. Forgive for not accepting the imperfect. Forgive for being neglected and treated unfairly. Forgive for not having an appreciation for the little things that matter most.

I can go on and on about a list of things we, as humans, fault ourselves for. When it comes down to it, most of those things don't even really matter. What does matter is the fact that God has forgiven us and has given all of us another chance. We must forgive others and ourselves because God died for our sins. He can make all things new and give us a fresh start!

Chapter 6

Broaden Your Horizon
& Share The Profit

When you have reached a point in your life where you are content, everything in your perspective becomes good. You have a peace from within that cannot and will not be disturbed. You know the one and only God who has your back.

You could have gone through the worst scenario and replay it multiple times in your mind, never really understanding the meaning behind all of it. It's easy to give up when you're weak and vulnerable, but when you are strong, confident, and sure, mix that with a bit of faith, hope, and desire. You know there is one you can call and count on. Oh, He will not leave you discombobulated and in distress. He will remind you to keep holding on and to know that "I AM GOD".

What does this mean? It is meant to encourage you to keep holding on because troubles don't last always. Keep holding on because in due season, things will change.

Keep holding onto what little bit of strength you have left. T.D. Jakes once said, "Don't let the devil or your circumstance fool you". This is not a setback, just a set up for what is ahead of you. Do not be dismayed. Joy comes in the morning.

A New Life

It is okay to be content in whatever state or season you are in. But don't be afraid to branch out and try something new. You never know what open door it will lead

—
59

you. Discover the possibilities that run through your mind. Let it soar into a journey of adventure. All things are possible through God for those who believe.

I think that exploring all of the options of something new is what helps build our character into an amazing and unique individual. We are able to cross our path in a better way of understanding what our purpose is. Doing something different can also teach to not be so worried about our everyday hectic lives and to make a conscious effort to help others in need.

There is no greater feeling than to have joy and peace in your heart, letting go and letting God lead you into something so divine. Walking out of what once was the ordinary helped me understand that

I had become a creature of habit. Now I'm looking to God for all of the answers. I'm looking to Him to make a way when there doesn't seem like one. I'm looking for peace of mind when I fall on hard times.

He is the only One who can deliver you from any situation that has turned into an unhealthy lifestyle. He is with us even in the midst of trials. But more importantly, He wants us to be an aid in our mission to make a difference in the world. By doing our part, supporting each other, lifting a hand, and sharing our testimony, we can change the world. We do these things in hopes that lives will be forever changed for His glory.

Remember to be open to new ideas and to walk with God each day. Ask Him to use the gifts He has given you to be used as a tool with a purpose in someone else's life. Additionally, always remember to *Never Retire God*!

About the Author

Donnetta Austin is from the Midwest. Her accomplishments include graduating from Scott Eastern Iowa Community College as a RDA registered dental assistant, CDA certified, and EFDA expanded functions dental assistant. She has worked in healthcare for eleven years. She also provides care for elderly as a nurse aide.

Donnetta enjoys writing inspirational books and feels this is part of her life's purpose. Her writing expresses the importance of living a life with no regrets, uplifting others, and making a significant impact by sharing her testimony. It is her life's goal to make a difference in the lives of others.

Contact Donnetta by e-mail at: be.encouragedbyone@gmail.com

Acknowledgements

First and foremost, I would like to thank God. Lord, this inspirational book would not have been possible without the blessing of you bringing life to it. Thank you for placing the desire on my heart to share "My Truth, My Story". Thank you for bringing forth your vision and guiding me step by step on how to live with purpose.

I would like to express my gratitude to my publisher, Kit Ford, and Testimonies of Hope Publishing. Thank you for this amazing life changing opportunity of being able to bless others through writing. My dream of publishing an inspirational book has come true!

www.ingramcontent.com/pod-product-compliance
Lightning Source LLC
Chambersburg PA
CBHW071852020426

42331CB00007B/1973